AT C

SPIRITUAL POETRY
FOR MIND, BODY AND SPIRIT

AT ONE

SPIRITUAL POETRY
FOR MIND, BODY AND SPIRIT

Anne Campbell

Dedicated to you

May these words written resonate with you and that you will always find peace and happiness in your life.

Always believe in miracles
because you are that miracle.

Acknowledgements

I don't want to come across as egotistical but I first want to thank myself. I want to say thank you to me for finding the courage and finally believing in myself to write this book. For many years I have hidden my passion because of fear of ridicule, but over time I have realised that I was born with my own unique gifts that I can share and I am forever grateful to myself for finally following my passion.

I also want to say a huge thank you to my husband and wonderful children who have given me support and encouragement to follow my dreams. They have always believed in me and it is with heartfelt gratitude that I write this book dedicating it them.

Table Of Contents

Preface 8

Piece By Piece 11

The Ripple Effect 12

Sands Of Time 16

Don't Judge Me 18

In The Eye Of The Beholder 20

The Voice Inside 22

Beliefs 24

Thoughts 26

Focus 28

Prayer 30

Forgiveness 32

Let Your Heart Lead The Way 34

Awakening 35

Letting Go 38

Its Already Yours 40

Letter To Heaven 41

Just As Autumn Proposed 43

Your Story	46
The Right Path	48
Good Morning	51
Last Breath	53
Meditation	54
I'm Possible	56
Your World	58

Preface

Ever since I can remember I have always had a fascination with the world that we live in. I used to ask countless questions about the universe, how we came to be and numerous "why" questions. That was over 30 years ago and we certainly did not have access to the abundance of information that we have at our finger tips today. My wonder and awe about the universe depleted as I matured and I conformed to the ideals and beliefs so that I could fit in with society.

That was until I was in my 30s. I started to become aware of the synchronicities in my everyday existence which prompted me to observe the events in my life and how material items seamlessly just appeared, granted sometimes I had to wait but I always received better than what I desired and it was always delivered to me in the best way possible. Stepping back from my daily slavery to society I started to join the dots of the matrix puzzle and realised that I had desired many of the things that appeared in my reality. I started seeking more about the truth of life and that is when I stumbled upon the book "The Secret". This book filled my heart with joy and it was almost as if my questions about the universe had been answered. It was as if this book was meant to find me and concrete my childhood beliefs.

My research did not stop there, I watched countless videos and read numerous books on the Law of Attraction, Mindfulness, breathing techniques and the functions of the heart and mind. Over the years I have realised that when we are aware and living fully in the present moment miraculous things happen in our lives. I have discovered that we create our own inner happiness and the outer environment that we live in is a reflection of our inner being. Trust me this has not been an easy process and I have had to do a lot of soul searching along the way as well as removing limiting beliefs which I have carried for many years. This journey of self discovery has had its ups and downs but I am grateful to have been on it. I am grateful for the wonderful things that have happened in my life and I am also thankful to the experiences that have proved not so favourable because I now realise that I was not in true alignment with my desires. This has then lead me on to believing that whatever you focus on matched with your inner state at that time inevitably becomes your reality.

My inspiration for this book has been through my observations of everyday people plus my own experiences throughout my life. I have subsequently combined this with my love of writing poetry and the laws of the universe to create the poems that I share with you.

Some of the poems may resonate with experiences in your own life and it is my aim that you will seek comfort in the knowing that there is always a way to get through the hurdles and obstacles that face us in life.

Piece By Piece

Life is like a jigsaw puzzle.
Fitting all the pieces together.
Some fit easily into place.
While others seem to take forever.

Starting at the bottom.
We create our perfect foundation.
Linking the pieces together.
Sometimes following tradition.

As we advance throughout our years.
We pick up pieces along the way.
Joining them to our creation of life.
In the hope they remain and stay.

Sometimes the pieces become distorted.
And no longer seem to fit.
We try our hardest to make them work.
But these ones we have to omit.

Interconnecting with all that surrounds.
Each individual section is a fraction of our existence.
And piece by piece a picture forms.
With our determination and persistence.

The Ripple Effect

When you drop a pebble into the river
it pushes the water away.
Symmetrical ripples effortlessly form.
A phenomenal sight to convey.

A ripple effect is created
from one drop in the vast expanse.
Expanding in ever increasing circles.
Whats happened is by no means chance.

And as that pebble falls deeper.
The water at the surface rushes back.
To fill the space left behind.
Facilely concealing its track.

In life see yourself as that pebble.
Whatever words or actions you take.
Will have a ripple effect on those around.
What decisions will you make?

Dropping the pebble of gossip
from those whom you take spite.
The ripples move from one to the next.
People will see you in a new light.

Dropping the pebble of anger.
As the frustration within you grows.
Picking and complaining about the small things.
The darkness inside you shows.

Dropping the pebble of selfishness
not willing to help others out.
But that effect will return one day.
When no one hears you shout.

Dropping the pebble of hatred
as you are engulfed with revenge and rage.
Seeking out to destroy others.
You will be imprisoned in your own cage.

Watch the pebbles the media hurl
and observe what they throw in.
Copious pebbles of fear and death.
The ones of happiness spread thin.

So change the pebbles you drop in
and begin to see their effect.
Because when we throw in the right pebbles
the results will truly reflect.

Cast the pebble of hope
and spread the ripples of a wish fulfilled.
See the delight in those around.
Now is the time to rebuild.

Cast the pebble of belief.
Feeling confident in the knowing.
Accepting that it truly exists.
Even without physically showing.

Cast the pebble of passion.
Let the excitement expand out.
Feel the rush of anticipation.
Only happiness will come about.

Cast the pebble of expectation.
Feel peaceful and inspired.
Knowing it is already yours.
All that you have desired.

Cast the pebble of kindness.
In helping others in a wonderful way.
Your heart will sing with pride and joy.
A feeling that will always stay.

Cast the pebble of love.
Let the ripples spread through you.
Learn to love yourself unconditionally.
And more love you will accrue.

Cast the pebble of euphoria.
One of pure joy and elation.
This is the most wondrous of pebbles.
Let the ripples last for a duration.

Be mindful of the pebbles you throw.
They can have a huge ripple effect.
Create the most magnificent ripple.
One which will gain you love and respect.

Sands Of Time

As the grains of sand slowly pass on by.
Our life moves on in the blink of an eye.
For what we have just experienced is now in the past.
Nothing stands still, it's not built to last.

For existence is forever changing in ways not seen.
What happened a second ago has already been.
What is happening tomorrow, we just don't know.
It's only until the present that the reality begins to show.

But why do we live so much in our own past.
The pain that you relive is unsurpassed.
Feeling the same emotions each and every day.
The thoughts are relishing in negative play.

And we wonder why we keep getting more of what we don't want.
But that movie gets played over and it begins to haunt.
Then we try to play a different scene.
Of a future of ourselves that has not yet been.

'Things will be different when I have this in my existence"
It will bring me the happiness and freedom, just some assistance.
And the frustration begins to raise it's ugly head.
When everything is still the same when we rise from our bed.

We don't live in the past and the future has yet to appear.
The present is where we live let go of the fear.
Relax into the now and let the anxieties go.
Be at one with the universe and learn to go with the flow.

Don't Judge Me

Don't judge me because you don't know.
Where I have been and where I will go.
For I am me and I am enough.
My exterior may show that I am tough.

Don't judge me on how I look.
If I listen to certain music or read a specific type book.
What hobbies I do and what I like.
Whether its stamp collecting or riding a bike.

Don't judge me for the clothes I wear.
To be honest, I just don't care.
I might wear things not in fashion.
I am an individual and thats my passion.

Don't judge me for the style of my hair.
If its black brown, multi coloured or fair.
I have choices that I can make
and with this opportunity I will take.

Don't judge me for the colour of my skin.
It should only matter whats within.
As long as I do things out of love.
That is something I am surely proud of.

Don't judge me for what I believe.
What gives me the motivation in order to achieve.
I may choose angels, the universe or god.
Whatever I believe in, I am not flawed.

Don't judge me because I am unique.
I am strong, proud and certainly not weak.
Please accept who I choose to be.
So I can live a life that is happy and free.

In The Eye Of The Beholder

Beauty is in the eye of the beholder.
That is what they say.
When you look in the mirror.
Do you feel the same way?

Are you disgusted by your reflection?
Criticising every feature belonging to you.
Seeing all your negative traits.
From your narrow point of view.

Focusing on the lumps and bumps.
The imperfections and scars.
Comparing yourself to others.
Idols and superstars.

The lines and wrinkles grow deeper.
From the stresses and strains of life.
Not the body that you once knew.
The corruption has become rife.

As you stare back at you're being.
The tears roll down your face.
Why cant you love yourself.
Without feeling this disgrace.

But stop for just a moment.
Be brave and stand proud.
Search within your soul.
And affirm this out loud.

"I am me and thats enough.
I am beautiful today.
I am unique to this world.
Each and every way".

Smile back at yourself.
Look deep into your eyes.
See the beauty from within.
Not your egotistical lies.

So when you look in the mirror.
See your true worth unfold.
Stop all the self sabotage.
And be proud of the beauty you hold.

The Voice Inside

Wallowing in the shadows.
Lurking in the dark.
Ready to engulf like a fire.
With a switch of an ignition spark.

Always there whispering.
Saying what you think is true.
Repetitive phrases circulating.
Your words no longer new.

In times of wondrous delight.
You are loitering ready to destroy.
Intimations of negativity.
Using us as your own decoy.

You are meant to be there to protect.
Not to put in harms way.
But your incessant echoing.
Lets us believe what you say.

And so the constant thought.
Becomes an ingrained belief.
No matter how hard you try.
There seems no relief.

Of the constant pain conjuring.
The entire day consumed.
No longer a magnificent flower.
But a noxious weed in the doomed.

And you long to be free like a bird.
From that voice in your head.
Dictating the thoughts you should think.
Which fill you with turmoil and dread.

But, it's not until its recognised.
The pattern consistently occurring.
And to become fully present.
Of the thoughts that are always stirring.
Catch them, observe them,
let them fully go.
Don't even focus on them.
Don't give them a chance to grow.

Prevent the vines of negativity
From hooking to your thoughts.
Cut all associations.
Unravel the entwined knots.

Beliefs

A belief is accepting that something exists
or knowing that something is true.
What beliefs are you carrying around?
Do they align with the truth in you?

As a child we get taught so much.
From many different sources.
Things we learn throughout our lives.
Sets us up in our future courses.

Beliefs can be positive or negative.
Empowering or destructive too.
But as we develop throughout our lives.
Our beliefs will stick like glue.

We may carry beliefs about ourselves.
Thinking we are not good enough.
Limiting our own possibilities.
Not seeing the diamond in the rough.

But once you become aware of your beliefs.
You will see what has been repressed.
The fire of disbelief will become extinguished.
And you will discover you are truly blessed.

Remove all the beliefs that do not serve you.
Embrace them, forgive them and let them go.
Transform your inner being.
And let your light begin to show.

Create new beliefs that will steer you in the right direction
To achieving love, happiness and true success.
You deserve the best in this life.
Walk your path with passion and finesse.

<u>Thoughts</u>

Start with a thought and like a seed.
Plant it and let it grow.
Nurture and care for this precious thought.
Until it begins to show.

In that garden of your mind.
Don't let the weeds come through.
Your ego will put doubts in your mind.
It will try to stop the new.

So if the doubts start creeping in.
Take a breath a clear your mind.
Analyse what weeds crop up.
Take the negative out and leave them behind.

When you nurture your thought like a seed.
Give it love straight from the heart.
Align your emotions and visualise.
This is where it will begin to start.

That tiny thought from within your head.
Will only grow in size.
Focus on the positive outcome
and soon you will realise.

Your thoughts become your reality.
So be careful what you choose.
Be that courageous winner in life.
The one that goes out and pursues.

The dream that you most desire.
For the greater good of all.
Remember that you can dream big.
You don't have to keep it small.

So now release your thought.
Believe and know its true.
Take action towards your goals and dreams.
Stay with it and see it through.

Focus

What would your ideal life be?
Is it lounging on a sun drenched beach.
Surrounded by crystal clear sea.
Or travelling first class to see new sights.
Exploring far distant lands.
Bustling cities with dazzling lights.
Or sampling the most exquisite of fare.
Shopping in exclusive boutiques.
Purchasing elegant wear.
Or having the freedom to choose how you live.
Your opulent, lavish lifestyle.
Allows you to share and give.
Or living a life of grandeur and wealth.
Happiness, love, laughter
and extremely good health.
Or pursuing a career that you love to do.
Using your true skills and talents.
Effortlessly being in alignment with you.
Or sharing precious moments with those that you love.
Creating new exciting experiences.
Doing the things you have dreamed of.

Or do you believe that you can't have all this.
That you are not worthy.
Of living a life of freedom and bliss.
Do you focus on all the hurt and the pain.
Of events that are in the past.
Feeling as if life will never be the same again.
Living your life in a constant state of want.
Emphasising on the lack in your life.
This hardship will only begin to taunt.
One day you will realise you will just get more.
Of the misery, sadness, negativity.
And not the things you truly adore.
Staring now live your life in a new fashion.
Focus with intent on your true self.
And begin to follow your dreams with passion.
Clear the negativity out of your head.
Release those old limiting beliefs.
Create new positive ones instead.
Vision your life the way you desire.
Arouse it with joyous emotion.
Take inspired action to achieve and acquire.

Prayer

Tumbling to the ground like a leaf swept off the trees.
She prayed to the angels above as she fell on bended knees.

Her tears like pearls cascaded from her pools of salted water.
She wasn't just a person, she was someones daughter.

She clasped her hands like a clam shut tight.
And tried to clear her mind with all her God given might.

The fear and pain starved her whole entire existence.
There was nothing left, there was no subsistence.

And the words of her plea poured out like water from a fountain.
Searching for the solution to climb life's monumental mountain.

Releasing the bottled up pain, she began to feel some relief.
For the first time ever, there seemed to be hope and belief.

And she raised her bowed head and looked up to the sky.
She said "Thank You for listening", yet did not expect a reply.

And a feeling of calmness washed over her entire physique.
She felt the chains had been severed, she was no longer weak.

Forgiveness

We have all made mistakes in life.
It's how we learn and grow.
But it is how you deal with these mistakes.
Will determine how you flow.

Each time that you bear a grudge.
You are bringing up the past.
You are reliving the errors that were made
and these will surely last.

Your vibration will be low.
With feelings that you don't want.
The guilt, the shame the hatred.
Will all begin to taunt.

You will feel a heavy burden.
Carried each and every day.
That churning in your stomach.
Will it ever go away?

The negative thoughts that consume you.
Will constantly replay in your mind.
Living in the past every single day.
This needs to be realigned.

So stop for just one moment
and spend some time to forgive.
Forgive yourself and others.
To enable you to move on and begin to live.

When we learn to forgive whats been done.
It allows you to flow with life.
Surrender all to the universe.
You don't need to live with this strife.

So with that lesson that you have learnt.
Move on and don't look back.
Hold on to your happy thoughts
and know you are on the right track.

Please learn to forgive yourself
And others around you too.
If you keep holding onto the past.
You can't let in the new.

Let Your Heart Lead The Way

It is your immense life force that does not criticise or judge in anyway.
It's goodness comes direct from source, its with you every moment of the day.

Your heart is pure and at the centre of your spirituality.
It is your true being and part of your individuality.

Very often we allow our mind to take control and mask our true existence.
We don't take time to listen to our heart and we put up a resistance.

Close your eyes and clear the clutter from your mind.
Listen to the beating of your heart and once again become aligned.

Awakening

The story I am about to tell you is all about me.
How my life began consuming negativity.
For as hard as I tried I could not shift.
The pressures of life that I wanted to lift.

The fear grew stronger every single day
as I focused my energy directly it's way.
I thought constantly about how things could go wrong.
I was consumed in darkness, I lost my beautiful song.

The churning in my stomach, the pain in my heart.
Why was it happening, why did it start?
I was blinded by the thoughts I was thinking.
I couldn't make the connection, I felt that I was sinking.

Each day the torture grew more and more.
I lost sight of all the things I used to adore.
I felt useless and worthless with no more to give.
I just wanted to be happy, I just wanted to live.

This went on for months and whatever I tried.
Nothing would shift the pain inside.
The pain that I was consistently feeding
and the negativity in my life kept on repeating.

I tried praying to angels and used affirmations.
Whatever I tried I could not shift my vibrations.
The more I prayed and the more I said.
My ego was relishing with the negativity in my head.

And the universe gave me more and more.
Of all the things I didn't adore.
I would sit for hours in floods of tears.
Just wishing someone would erase my fears.

My exterior did not reflect the horror inside.
I felt my whole life was crumbling, I had no where to hide.
There were signs guiding me every single day.
But my focus was directed in the opposite way.

Then one day I thought enough was enough.
I decided inside that I had to get tough.
I had to take control of my spiralling life.
To heal myself from this horrendous strife.

The very next morning I saw this book in plain sight.
It seemed to be illuminated by the sunlight.
I sat down and read it from cover to cover.
I was so intrigued, there was much to discover.

I had read these types of books many times in the past.
I would practice the theories but nothing would last.
But this one book put in the simplest of form.
Was the sunlight amidst my tempestuous storm.

In what seemed like an instant, I let the negativity go.
I felt the lightness encase my body, I felt I was in the flow.
Of pure joy and bliss that filled my heart.
I knew this was a chance of a new start.

I decided that day that a miracle had occurred.
To those around that might seem absurd.
But I promised myself that I wouldn't look back.
Living a life in fear and in lack.

I was writing my life story out of fear and lack.
And the universe was obedient and gave exactly that back.
That book made me realise that I had everything and more.
I was surrounded by all the things I did actually adore.

The answers I had been seeking were with me all along.
I discovered myself again, I had found my beautiful song.
I saw my life in a completely new light.
I was truly abundant and my heart was full of delight.

I focus my energy on the beauty of each day.
Giving the universe thanks along the way.
And I say to myself "I have more than enough.
I am living my dream life now, the one that I love"

Letting Go

Its time for me to let you go.
How will I survive, I don't know.
You have been part of my life for so long.
Keeping you in my existence is so wrong.

I have fear that I can't survive.
But you are not what keeps me alive.
Without you I am much better off.
You choke me like an irritating cough.

In my thoughts frequently every day.
You break me down, I'm starting to decay.
Cravings running deep to my core.
I can't take this anymore.

You make me feel sick to the pit of my soul.
When I eradicate you I will climb out of this hole.
You have controlled my every move.
I know I can do this without you, that I will prove.

You fooled me into thinking that you were my friend.
But that friendship has to finally come to an end.
I see you as my enemy from this point on.
I have had enough, I just want you gone.

The veil of illusion you tricked me with.
I am worth more, I have so much to give.
And I am capable without you smothering me.
I will fly high like a bird for all to see.

I will not let you shackle me to your invisible chains.
I love my life too much I can feel it running through my veins.
So I forgive myself for even entertaining you.
I will break these chains and make my debut.

It might take hours, days or weeks.
For me to overcome your hostile tweaks.
I am in control, I am stronger than you think.
I have made my decision, I have broken the link.

And now I stand here in this present moment in time.
I feel completely free and I feel utterly sublime.
I have put my self first no longer a slave.
Your incessant taunts I no longer crave.

Its Already Yours

The universe is listening to each thought and every desire.
When you add emotion, it ignites like a fire.
Ready to deliver just as you required.
Everything that you have wanted, will soon be acquired.

Whether it is positive intentions or those out of lack and fear.
The universe is listening and you must be very clear.
On the direction of your focus and where your attention goes.
The universe is obedient and will match where your energy flows.

Letter To Heaven

The day you left me
was the hardest day of all.
I pleaded and prayed so very hard.
But God did not hear my call.

You had so much to give.
You were the kindest person that I knew.
It just didn't seem fair
that God had chosen you.

He had chosen you to depart this world
and live in eternity.
I believe that you are in heaven
Watching over me.

And every day I think of you.
A warmth fills my heart.
For you were always my inspiration
right from the very start.

Glimpses of sweet memories
through the silent tears I've cried.
I don't feel alone anymore
knowing you will always be at my side.

And every night when I lay my head down
and close my eyes for sleep.
I see you in my dreams
that image I will forever keep.

I just want to say thank you
for all you did for me.
For showing me the ways of life
to live in peace and harmony.

And even though you are gone
you left footprints to guide me.
I will follow them the best I can
so that you can be proud of me.

I believe one day we will meet again
not on this earthly plane.
When I see you standing waiting for me.
We will embrace our love again.

Just As Autumn Proposed

The whispering wind rustled through the trees
and the leaves began to fall.
Tumbling, twirling and floating.
As autumn announced her call.

The layers of beauty begin to unfasten
and the bareness is exposed.
Flowers depleting daily.
Just as autumn had proposed.

Natures growing ever weary.
The summer cycle ends once more.
She shreds the once vibrant colours.
As golden hues blanket the floor.

Shadows fill the garden lawn.
Which was once filled with light.
Creeping and swallowing the lush green grass.
Under the darkness of her plight.

The autumn sun grows weaker.
Disappearing out of sight.
Falling ever faster.
As day quickly turns to night.

The clouds grow opaque and heavy.
The greyness fills the sky.
Rain becomes tempestuous.
As the calm days bid goodbye.

And the atmosphere grows colder.
As a chill fills the air.
Autumns winds are blowing.
Without a thought or care.

The hustle and bustle of insects.
And the sweet melody of song.
Are a rare sight to see and hear.
When autumn comes along.

But nature goes through cycles.
In such an effortless way.
Nothing ever stays the same.
It changes everyday.

This natural shift happens
to rest and rejuvenate.
To be prepared for the coming months.
In order to recreate.

And as autumn knocks upon our door.
Take time to reassess.
What layers do we need to shred.
To get back to our wholeness.

Lets take lessons from mother nature.
And observe what cycles we go through.
What should we discard from our lives.
In preparation for the new.

Your Story

Imagine for one moment that you could write your own story.
One full of amazement and filled with glory.
A story about your most perfect existence.
A wonderful life without insistence.

Would your life be a tale of action and adventure?
A life without fear to pursue your chosen venture.
To travel the world and see new sights.
To sample and taste wondrous delights.

Would your life be filled with love and romance?
With your perfect partner whom you met by chance.
Spending cosy evenings curled up close together.
Living in blissful peace and harmony forever.

Would you follow your true life passion?
Pursuing your career in the most amazing fashion.
Waking with enthusiasm each and every day.
Doing soul fulfilling work and receiving wonderful pay.

Would you live in a vibrant city or on a remote small isle?
One which suits your ideal lifestyle.
Whether it is the hustle and bustle and bright city lights.
Or living in isolation with the most awe inspiring sights.

You are the author of your own life book.
Open your eyes and take a look.
What has been the story that you have been writing.
Is it one that is joyful and exciting.

Every day is a chance to write a new chapter.
Believe in yourself you are a super attractor.
To have all that you desire in this universe.
Be independent and be utterly diverse.

The Right Path

I saw a person standing there.
They didn't seem to have a care.
About the world rushing by.
Then I heard them give a sigh.

The sigh they gave was from the heart.
I didn't know where to start.
Do I ask them if they are alright?
Or do I turn and take flight.

The thing is that we don't know.
Is how to act or how to show.
Our caring, loving nature at times.
To people that are in our lives.

But if that was me how would I feel?
If I needed someone there who's real.
To listen to my worries and fears.
And be there to prevent all my tears.

So I turned and said "let it all out".
"Do what you want cry or shout
Let me take the burden away
I will listen to each word you say".

"Don't think bad of me, please".
As their words flowed out with such ease.
Their hurt and suffering filled my ears.
They had suppressed this for many years.

They just needed to release the pain.
They just wanted to be free again.
Free to love, live and laugh.
To start a new life on the right path.

So with each word that was said to me.
There was a sense of urgency.
To let all this burden be lifted.
So that all their worry could be shifted.

I listened to every single word.
I want to free you like a bird
Caged in your torturous mind
Its time to leave all the suffering behind.

"You live in the now, the past has gone
You have been wounded far too long
Surrender all thats in your head
Let the universe deal with it instead".

"You will find the right path you know.
You will learn to love again and grow.
To be the person you are meant to be.
To live with joy and be free".

"Forgive yourself for your mistakes.
You are only human for goodness sakes.
Be thankful with an open heart.
That you have an opportunity to make a new start"

Focus on the here and now
Live each day and allow
Your heart to be filled with so much love
To receive loving messages from above.

Good Morning

When you wake in the morning and open your eyes.
Take time to contemplate and to realise.
That you are alive to live another day.
Be grateful to the universe and take time to say.

Thank you for the air I breathe, for my taste, touch and sight.
Thank you for my being which is my true birthright.

Thank you for my family and the love that we all share.
Thank you for my friends who always seem to care.

Thank you for the food I eat and the water that runs free.
Thank you for the shops that provide it fresh for me.

Thank you for the farmers, the factory workers too.
Thank you for the teachers and all the work they do.

Thank you for the emergency services, who keep us safe and secure.
Thank you for the artists who inspire us for sure.

Thank you for the birds that sing their sweet melody.
Thank you for the grass, flowers and the buzzing of a bee.

Thank you for the insects that dispose of all the waste.
Thank you for the entire ecosystem which is perfectly placed.

Thank you for the glorious sun that gives us warmth and light.
Thank you for the moon that lights up the darkened night.

Thank you for the magnificence of the twinkling shining stars.
Thank you for the wonderful plants like Jupiter and Mars.

Thank you for today a new start in my existence.
Thank you for being always there for assistance.

When you say thank you for the things in your life it can be anything you adore.
Family, friends, material items you will appreciate so much more.
When you give gratitude in the morning it sets you up for the day.
You will soon begin to realise that you are blessed in every way.

Thank you!

Last Breath

Why do you take me for granted?
I sustain your whole life.
If it wasn't for me where would you be?
You wouldn't be alive.

Why do you take me for granted?
Every second of the day.
You just expect it of me.
Not showing gratitude in anyway

Now you don't take me for granted.
As you struggle for your last breath.
Hoping and praying for one more sigh.
Before the inevitable death.

Meditation

Focus upon your breath that keeps you alive each day.
Calm the chatter in your head, only observe what it is trying to say.
Breathe in love and breath out what you need to release.
Feel your body relax and become easily at peace.

Staring from your toes, feel the sensation.
Of the energy in your body, your essential vibration.
Working up your legs detecting the power starting to move.
Feeling ever more relaxed as the energy begins to soothe.

Up to your body encompassing you're being.
This force flows through you without you physically seeing.
Down along your arms to your finger tips.
Then up through your shoulders, your neck and then to your lips.

Feel the energy tingle as it moves through your head.
Keep concentrating on you're breathing not what your ego has said.
Then from the top of your head visualise a beam of light and observe how it flows.
Notice the gentle sensation encompass you as the healing energy grows.

Deep breath in and then out as your mind remains unstirring.
Sense your body become lighter the magic is occurring.
And you enter a point of no space or time.
As you embrace the emptiness and peace you will feel in your prime.

Continue concentrating on your breath if your mind starts to drift.
And gently guide yourself back to this wondrous spiritual gift.
The stillness you feel means that you are aligned.
As the swirls of darkness encompass your mind.

And at this point of complete calm and tranquility.
You become one with source, you are in complete unity.

I'm Possible

Thats impossible, I can't do that, it's not for me.
I will pass today, give it away.
To someone who is not a nobody.

Thats impossible I don't have the determination or will.
I am safe here, without the fear.
I will take a step back and chill.

Thats impossible, maybe I will start tomorrow.
It's only a day, it will fleet away.
I can't cope with pain or sorrow.

Thats impossible, I will never fulfil my dreams.
Who would even look at me, take me seriously.
I will stay behind the scenes.

Thats impossible, I don't have the confidence or flair.
I am comfortable being invisible.
I don't want people to stare.

Thats impossible, who would love someone like me.
With low self esteem, I can only dream.
Of a life being blissfully happy.

But what if that impossible turned to I'm possible.
I am capable, totally unshakeable.
I can also be unstoppable.

I'm possible, someone could easily love me.
I have high self esteem, I allow myself to dream.
I can live a life being blissfully happy.

I'm possible, I do have confidence and flair.
I stand here proud because I am allowed.
I don't care if people do stare.

I'm possible, I can fulfil my dreams.
Someone will notice me, take me seriously.
I won't hide behind the scenes.

I'm possible, I can start right now.
Todays the day, I won't let it fleet away.
I can do this somehow.

I'm possible I have the determination and will.
I will step out of my comfort zone, I know I'm not alone.
I have an abundance of natural talent and skill.

I'm possible, I can do that, thats definitely for me.
I will do it today, I won't give it away.
I am creating my new reality.

Your World

The world you live in.
Is full of wonder and awe.
Pause for a minute.
Look at the things you adore.
Whether it is the house you live in.
Your children playing with glee.
Be thankful for your life.
Open your eyes to see.
The wonders you have created.
With your own fair hand.
You have abundance in your life.
These were dreams that were once planned.

My thought became my reality
and so can yours.

Thank you!

Printed in Great Britain
by Amazon